The Snake Under Grandma's Couch

By Jennie Lawrence

Illustrated by Madora Daley-Green

Pendragon Publishing, LCC
P.O. Box 893
Laramie, WY 82073
PendragonPublishingLLC@gmail.com.

ISBN (paperback): 979-8-9860410-4-9
Library of Congress control number

Illustrated by Madora Daley-Green

100% Human Created Content - No AI

Printed in the United States

In memory of
Aunt Donna and her imaginary friends.

"Do we have to go see Grandma?" Jason grumbled as his dad steered the car into the assisted living home parking lot.

"Yes, we have to see Grandma. Your mother and I haven't been here for two weeks, and you haven't been in over a month. It is important that we visit her regularly."

"But sometimes she doesn't even know my name," Jason whined. "She calls me Davey. I don't even know who Davey is!"

"I know, son. Davey was my nickname when I was a boy. You look a lot like I did when I was your age. Grandma thinks you are me when I was a little boy."

Jason's dad pulled the car into a parking space behind the retirement home. One whole row of the parking lot was nothing but blue parking spots. The old people who still drove cars got to park closest to the building.

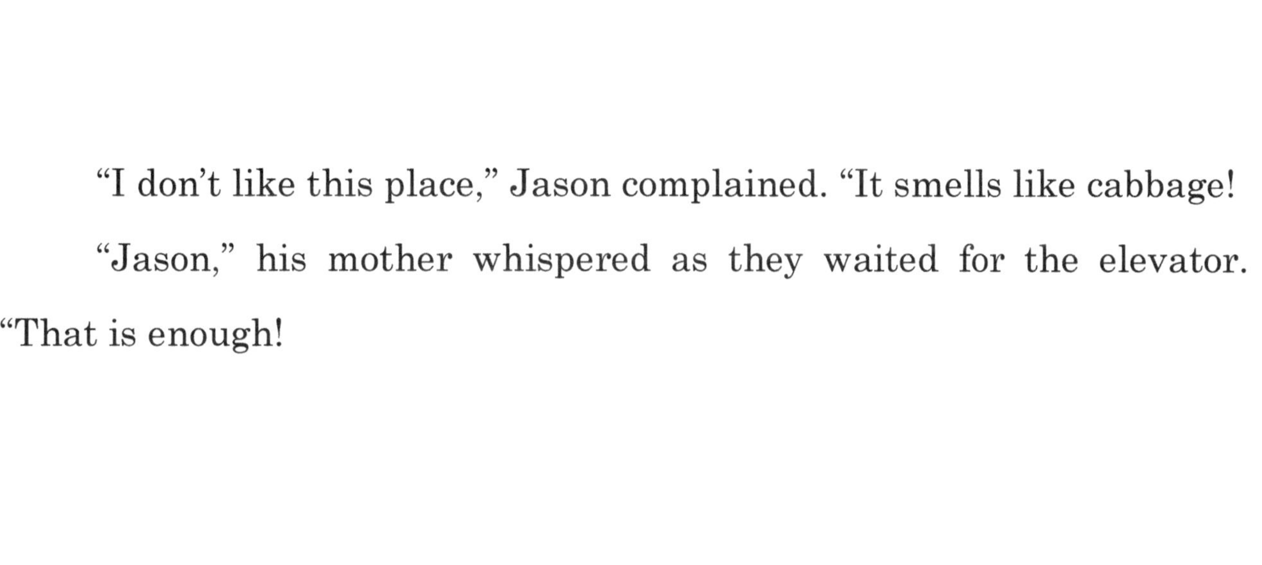

"I don't like this place," Jason complained. "It smells like cabbage!

"Jason," his mother whispered as they waited for the elevator. "That is enough!

The family entered the elevator, joining a gray-haired lady using a walker.

"Aren't you just the cutest little boy?" She patted Jason on the head.

Jason did not say a word until they were off the elevator at the second floor.

They walked through the television lounge where a group of old people was gathered. The senior citizens called out to the family.

"Good afternoon!"

"Hello there, young lad!"

"Who are you here to visit?"

As soon as they were past the lounge, Jason grumbled again. "I don't like it when they touch me and talk to me. I don't even know any of these people except Grandma."

"Jason," his mother sighed. "They are going to talk to you. Many people here do not have visitors, even on holidays. They like to see different faces, especially kids. They probably have grandchildren of their own that they don't get to see very often. That is why they like seeing you. But we can ask them not to touch you."

"I still don't like it!"

"You'll understand when you are older about them being glad to see you. One day when I was here by myself, they asked me if I was the teacher. I guess Grandma told them what I do for my job. I told them I was, and then I had to settle an argument about a town! "

Jason's dad stopped in front of Grandma's door and rang the doorbell. The nurse's assistant answered.

"Dave, Nancy, Jason! Clara will be delighted to see you. I told her you were coming."

Grandma Clara sat in her chair, a breakfast tray on her lap. Her wavering voice greeted them with excitement.

"Come in! Have you had breakfast? Candy, do we have any more of these things?" She gestured with her bagel.

"We're fine," Jason's mom said. "We ate breakfast before we left."

"I thought you probably had," The nurse's aide reassured Clara.

"Sit down, sit down," Grandma said.

Jason started to sit on the couch.

"You be careful, Davey! There is a snake under the couch!" Grandma whispered loudly.

Jason leaped to his feet. "What? There is a snake under your couch?" he exclaimed.

"Oh, yes," Grandma said with a big smile on her face.

"Mom, remember I threw the snakes out the window?" Jason's dad calmly reminded her.

"I know, but it was cold, and one came back in." Grandma frowned.

Jason was very confused. He looked from his dad to his grandma, and then back again. His dad caught Jason's eye and gave him The Look. Jason knew better than to say another word.

"You can sit there, Davey. Just be careful of my friend." Grandma spoke softly.

Jason looked at his father. His dad nodded his head. Jason eased himself onto the couch, careful not to sit down hard.

"So, there is a snake under the couch?" Jason's mom turned to Grandma.

"Yes. But he is a nice snake. Sometimes he comes out and sits up and looks at me."

"Uh huh," Jason's mom said. "I am glad he is a nice snake."

"This is really creepy," Jason thought to himself, pulling his feet up off the floor, just in case the snake slithered out.

The rest of the day went like it always did when they went to visit Grandma. They sat around and talked, then went to a restaurant downtown for lunch, and then they went back to Grandma's apartment and sat around some more.

Jason wished he had brought a video game to play, or at least a book to read. He thought about looking for the snake. Maybe that would be exciting.

Instead, he had to listen to the adults talk. This time it was different because sometimes Grandma made sense, and other times she didn't. She saw a hummingbird inside the china cabinet.

At first, Jason was excited and jumped up to look. He couldn't see the hummingbird. Then Grandma said there were people floating in and out of the walls. Jason got scared again.

He was glad when they finally left, even though Grandma hugged him and kissed him and wouldn't let go.

Jason looked out the window as his dad pulled the car onto the highway. He was thinking about Grandma and all the other old people. His father noticed.

"What are you thinking about, son?"

"I guess I don't get why Grandma thinks a snake lives under the couch and hummingbirds are in the china cabinet, and why there are people there that we can't see."

His father thought for a moment. "Remember when you were little? You had that imaginary friend Stevie?"

Jason agreed.

"Well," explained his father. "Sometimes when people get old, their brains start playing tricks on them. They see things that aren't there, or they think people they knew a long time ago are there. The things they see and the people they talk to are very real in their minds. That is what has happened to Grandma. Sometimes she will know who we are and sometimes she won't. But we will keep coming to see her because we love her."

Jason sat quietly, thinking about what his father said.

"I will never understand this, even when I am older," he thought. Then he remembered something. Stevie always made him feel better. He was never lonely when Stevie was around. He always had someone to play with.

"Maybe," Jason thought, "that is the way it is with Grandma and the other old people. Maybe this way they aren't lonely."

Jason hoped that the snake was keeping Grandma company. That way she wouldn't be lonely until he could visit her again.

ABOUT THE AUTHOR

Jennie was born in Boulder, Colorado. She moved to Wyoming as a young adult and has called it home since. She attended the University of Wyoming, and has degrees in Agricultural Communications, and Education.

Jennie is a retired high school science teacher. She is a Certified Wyoming Naturalist and enjoys teaching students of all ages about nature and the world around us.

Jennie loves to hear from her readers. You can sign up for her newsletter at www.jennielawrence.com

Follow me on social media!

Facebook JenniferLawrenceAuthor

Instagram missjennie.author

Webpage jennielawrence.com

To order bulk copies of *The Snake Under Grandma's Couch*, contact Jennie through any of these social media sites.

Also By the Author

Soap Suds Row The Bold Lives of Army Laundresses, 1802-1876 (winner of the 2017 WILLA Scholarly Non-Fiction Award)

Horsethief Moon: An Abby and Maddie Mystery Book (ages 9-13)